CINDERELLA

Once upon a time, there was a rich merchant and his wife. They lived happily with their daughter until, one day, the merchant's wife became very ill and died. After a while, however, the merchant married again. His new wife brought her two daughters with her and the three of them were very cruel to the merchant's daughter.

When the merchant was away on business they made his daughter work like a servant. One of her jobs was to clean out the kitchen fireplace and because she was often covered in cinders from the fire, her stepsisters called her Cinderella.

Poor Cinderella had to work from morning till night, cleaning the kitchen, cooking, scrubbing the floors, dusting, polishing and washing the clothes. She was given old clothes to wear and made to sleep in the attic. Her stepsisters,

however, were able to buy fine clothes and they would spend hours in their elegant bedrooms looking at themselves in the mirrors. Yet no matter what they wore or how many lotions they applied to their faces, they were both very ugly. They were jealous of Cinderella, because she looked far prettier than them. Her curly hair framed a delicate face with big, blue, sparkling eyes and a gentle mouth. While both stepsisters had pale, dull skin that was often covered in spots

and lumps, Cinderella's skin was as soft as a peach and her cheeks a rosy pink.

The cruel stepsisters took great delight in teasing Cinderella as she worked.

'Come on, Cinderella,' one of them jeered. 'You're not working fast enough.'

'Here's a bit you missed,' called the other, as she rubbed her dirty shoe on a clean tile.

The stepsisters laughed and giggled, but Cinderella worked on quietly. When her father returned from his trips abroad, she did not tell him what happened for fear of upsetting him. Her stepmother took good care to be especially nice to her husband so that he would think she was always kind and generous to his daughter.

As she grew up Cinderella had to work harder and harder. Yet all the time she grew more beautiful and this made the stepsisters very angry. They complained about her to their mother.

One day, when Cinderella had finished her work and was sitting quietly in a corner, her stepmother came past with a handful of peas. 'What do you think you are doing?' she asked. 'I did not say you could sit down.'

'But I have finished my work for today,' said Cinderella.

'Well, here's another job for you!' exclaimed her mean stepmother, and she threw the peas all over the floor. 'Pick up those peas and clean the floor again. Look, it's dirty.' The wicked stepmother trod on some of the peas so that they were ground into the floor, and walked out of the room.

Cinderella gathered up the peas into her apron. She tried

hard not to cry, but a few tears fell from her eyes and she sighed, 'I wish I could run away and marry a prince.'

Just then, there was a loud knock at the front door and standing outside was a man from the King's household who handed the maid a sealed envelope.

Inside the envelope was an invitation from the King to

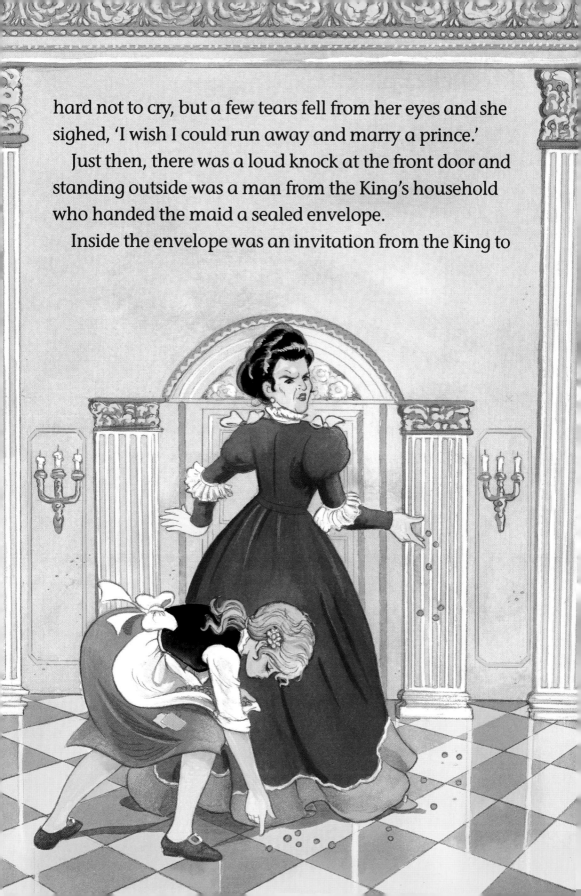

a ball in honour of his son, the Prince! The whole family was invited. The stepsisters were delighted, but the older girl said at once, 'Well, Cinderella can't go. She would make everyone feel ill with her ugly face and dirty clothes!'

The other stepsister laughed and they ran up to their bedrooms to plan their new ballgowns. The stepmother went to the kitchen to tell Cinderella about the invitation.

'But you will have to stay here,' she said. 'I'll give you plenty of jobs to do so that you aren't bored.'

Cinderella shed bitter tears. It seemed her whole life would be spent doing dirty, tiring household chores.

The evening of the ball arrived and Cinderella sat alone in the kitchen. She was just thinking how unlucky she was when, in a sudden flash of light, a fairy appeared before her! 'I am your fairy godmother and I am going to see to it that you go the Prince's ball,' she said.

Cinderella gasped. She could not believe her eyes. The fairy told her to fetch a pumpkin, six mice and two lizards.

When Cinderella had found these things, the fairy took the

pumpkin and waved her magic wand over it. To Cinderella's surprise it turned into a magnificent carriage. Next, the fairy godmother changed the mice into a team of horses to pull the carriage. She turned the lizards into two smart uniformed footmen.

The fairy turned to Cinderella, 'And now for you,' she laughed, as she waved her magic wand. In a flash, Cinderella's ragged clothes had turned into a beautiful ballgown and her dirty old shoes had become delicate glass slippers.

'How can I thank you?' Cinderella gasped in delight.

Her fairy godmother smiled and said, 'You have deserved this for being so hardworking and patient with your stepmother and stepsisters. Now, I want you to promise me that you will leave the ball at midnight, because this is when my magic spell will come to an end.'

Cinderella promised to do as the fairy had said, then she jumped into the carriage which took her straight to the royal palace.

When she arrived at the palace, the guards thought she was a princess and showed her to the ballroom. As soon as the Prince saw her, he fell in love with her and asked her to dance. Cinderella danced so gracefully and was so beautiful that the Prince did not want to dance with anyone else. The other guests, including the stepmother and ugly sisters, wondered who this entrancing stranger could be. The ugly sisters were jealous of her beauty and they were cross that the Prince did not ask them to dance. Indeed, the Prince did not

notice any of the other young ladies in the room as he had eyes only for his mysterious dancing partner.

'Tell me your name,' the Prince begged Cinderella.

But Cinderella would not tell him her name nor where she came from. However, the Prince was so enchanted with her that he would not let her out of his sight for an instant.

The King could see that his son had found the girl he wanted to marry and he tried to find out more about the beautiful stranger, but nobody at the ball knew anything about her.

The evening flew by for Cinderella, who was just as much in love with the Prince as he with her. She was dancing to a waltz with him when, to her horror, she heard the clock begin to strike midnight. All of a sudden she remembered the promise she had made to her fairy godmother and she tore herself from the Prince's grasp. She ran out of the ballroom and down some steps. In her haste, however, she stumbled and lost one of her glass slippers.

The Prince, who was running after her, stopped to pick up the glass slipper and when he looked up, Cinderella had gone. She had run among some bushes and was completely hidden when, on the last stroke of midnight, her dress turned into the rags and tatters she had worn before. Poor Cinderella had to walk all the way home and she only just had time to put on another pair of shoes before her stepmother and ugly sisters returned.

All three of them were in bad moods and ordered her to run here and there to fetch hot water and help them undress. The stepmother had hoped that the Prince would pick one of her daughters for his bride while the other would find a rich nobleman to marry. The ugly sisters, however, had not danced with anyone and they were angry with the Prince for choosing to dance with a stranger.

They tried to make Cinderella jealous by telling her that the Prince had told them they were beautiful. But Cinderella knew this was not true and, tired as she was, she could not help smiling at their silly stories. When the

stepsisters saw her smiling they grew even angrier and more spiteful. Poor Cinderella had to stay up all night doing chores that could have waited until the next day. She was filled with happy thoughts as she remembered the wonderful time she had had at the ball and how the handsome Prince had chosen to dance with her.

Meanwhile, at the King's palace, the Prince wanted to know what had become of his mysterious dancing partner. The gardens were searched thoroughly and the guards were questioned about who they had seen leaving the grounds. No one had seen the girl pass through the gates and the Prince despaired of ever finding her again.

At last, the Prince thought of a plan to find his beloved princess. He would take the glass slipper to each household in

the land and every young girl had to try it on. He would
marry the girl whose foot fitted exactly into the glass slipper.

At last the Prince came to Cinderella's house. The ugly
sisters tried on the slipper. It was far too small for one of them
and far too narrow for the other. The Prince was about to
leave when one of his servants, who had a list of all the girls
in the land, asked to see the other daughter of the house. The
wicked stepmother told them not to bother with Cinderella,

but the Prince insisted and Cinderella came out to try on the glass slipper.

It fitted her foot perfectly and everyone was astonished. The Prince asked Cinderella if she had been at the ball. She told him the whole story and he was overjoyed. 'I have found my wife,' he declared.

Cinderella went with the Prince to the royal palace where they were married and lived happily ever after.